The Paris Letter

By the same author

JON ROBIN BAITZ

The Paris Letter

A Play in Two Acts

Grove Press
New York

Published simultaneously in Canada
Printed in the United States of America

FIRST EDITION

Library of Congress Cataloging-in-Publication Data

Baitz, Jon Robin, 1961-
    The Paris letter : a play in two acts / John Robin Baitz.—1st ed.
      p. cm.
    ISBN-10: 0-8021-4246-X
    ISBN-13: 978-0-8021-4246-7
    1. Gay men—Drama.   2. Closeted gays—Drama.   3. Wall Street (New York, N.Y.)—Drama.   I. Title.
    PS3552.A393P37 2006
    812'.54—dc22   2005052548

Grove Press
an imprint of Grove/Atlantic, Inc.
841 Broadway
New York, NY 10003

06 07 08 09 10   10 9 8 7 6 5 4 3 2 1

To IVA
A most perfect friend

ACKNOWLEDGMENTS

The Paris Letter was first given a workshop reading at the 2002 Ojai Playwrights Festival. The cast was Ron Rifkin, Dana Delany, Daniel Davis, Will McCormack, and Jonathan Woodward. All were generous with time and ideas. It was directed by Michael Morris, who also directed the Los Angeles production. To Michael I owe a profound debt of gratitude for his vast generosity, his insight, and his boundless enthusiasm.

A playwright depends on the kindness of producers, and I would be remiss not to thank Nicky Martin at the Huntington, who commissioned the play; Robert Egan, the artistic director of the Ojai Festival; and Gordon Davidson of the Mark Taper Forum in Los Angeles, who is a friend and a hero to so many in the American theatre. He has supported and believed in my work over the course of two happy decades. I grew up going to his theatre, and I was very proud that *The Paris Letter* was included in his last season at the Taper. He created a slot for us in a season that had no slots, and did so without hesitation. Thanks also are due to Todd Haimes of the Roundabout, and to Doug Hughes for his beautiful production there.

I would also like to acknowledge the influence of essayist Alix Spiegel, for her radio piece for NPR's *This American Life,* entitled "81 Words," which details how the American Psychiatric Association decided, in 1973, that homosexuality was no longer an illness. Martin Duberman's classic and elegant book *Cures* and Charles Kaiser's crystalline *The Gay Metropolis* proved invaluable in researching gay life in New York over the past several decades. Finally, I would also like to thank Joe Mantello, who knows exactly how to look at a play lovingly and critically, and Jay Huguley, for his laughter and his kindness.

The Paris Letter was commissioned and developed by Huntington Theatre Company, Boston—Nicholas Martin, artistic director, Michael Maso, managing director—through the Stanford Calderwood Fund for New American Plays.

The Paris Letter had its world premiere at Center Theatre Group's (Gordon Davidson, artistic director) Kirk Douglas Theatre in Los Angeles on December 5, 2004. It was directed by Michael Morris, the set design was by Michael Brown, costume design was by Alex Jaeger, lighting design was by Christopher Akerlind, sound design was by Adam Phalen, and original music was by Nathan Wang. The cast was as follows:

SANDY SONNENBERG, DR. MORITZ SCHIFFMAN Ron Rifkin

ANTON KILGALLEN Lawrence Pressman

BURT SARRIS, YOUNG ANTON Neil Patrick Harris

SAM, YOUNG SANDY Josh Radnor

KATIE ARLEN, LILLIAN SONENBERG Patricia Wettig

The Paris Letter then had its New York City premiere at the Roundabout Theatre Company's (Todd Haimes, artistic director) Laura Pels Theatre on May 13, 2005. It was directed by Doug Hughes, the set design was by John Lee Beatty, costume design was by Catherine Zuber, lighting design was by Peter Kaczorowski, and sound design and original music were by David Van Tieghem. The cast was as follows:

SANDY SONNENBERG, DR. MORITZ SCHIFFMAN Ron Rifkin

ANTON KILGALLEN John Glover

BURT SARRIS, YOUNG ANTON Jason Butler Harner

SAM, YOUNG SANDY Daniel Eric Gold

KATIE ARLEN, LILLIAN SONENBERG Michele Pawk

WAITER Christopher Czys

The Paris Letter

ACT ONE

Two men kissing. Or are they fighting? One is sixty-some years old, exquisitely dressed, his back to us, the other is half his age, in underwear and T-shirt. BURT SARRIS, the younger man, has been crying. SANDY SONNENBERG, the older one, tries to pull away. They struggle. Then the passion reignites. Some sense of the cavernous expanse of a loft—a large painting in the back and a red metal spiral staircase leading up into the dark, way upstage.

BURT *(desperate)* Please, Sandy, listen to me, please, trust me, I can fix it, I still can. There's still time . . .

SANDY *(pulls away, gasping)* It's no good, it can't work anymore, that's no good . . .

BURT Please, Sandy, we have to talk . . . you can't leave it like this.

SANDY I don't think either of us understand what's happened here, Burt. *(beat)* The ramifications.

BURT Yes, it's all in my name. I'm the one they write about . . . ! *The Wall Street Journal* is calling me a pirate!

SANDY Your name wouldn't—what would your name be—I'm sorry but your name meant nothing! You're just another penny-ante, three-card-monte-hustling, arriviste faggot—I had two generations of—

BURT *(bellowing)* My name is my name! It's all I've got. I have parents! I have—*(beat)*

SANDY How could—was I insane—tell me what happened, explain to me . . . ?

3

BURT You wanted me to make more money for your people! You told me to! High risk, high return, just to let you off the hook, and I did it!

SANDY There is a fortune vanished.

BURT No, you know it's not vanished, it's . . . I know what you must think but there's money, I have money! It's not all gone, we still . . . ?

SANDY Where?

BURT It's here.

He goes to a table, hands Sandy a notebook. Sandy reads, looks at numbers, shakes his head. Reads some more.

SANDY Where is this island of Naru?

BURT Nowhere. Somewhere between New Zealand and nowhere. It's a rock with a bank on it, and a guano pit.

SANDY Zurich, Lucerne, Cayman Islands . . . Burt.

BURT Listen to me. I have information. Listen to me. We could—I know for a fact that Meechum Pharmaceuticals is buying—for one thing—and my friend Travers—Travers works for the fed and he knows seven minutes beforehand when Greenspan is going to announce a—

SANDY Stop.

BURT They are being bought, I know this, I know it, I have followed them since two and a half years ago—

SANDY *(yelling)* Stop!

Burt puts on pants and a shirt; they have been discarded on the floor. He looks for his glasses, eventually finding them.

SANDY *(cont.) (scornfully)* Meechum Pharmaceuticals. You think I have bread pudding between my ears? *(He laughs.)* Before that it was . . . a macro-trader in Boston, someone who you adored for European bonds, another fellow for Japanese distressed securities . . .

Burt sits down in the Eames chair.

BURT This year has been bad. You knew, I checked with you.

SANDY How come all this money is sitting in these banks? In Bora-Bora and so on. I never quite took you for a thief, I thought you were just insanely reckless, but really, you were simply insane.

BURT I got in trouble and when some of my people started to bolt, I had to come up with their money quickly and—it was plugging holes. It was plugging holes. And then the dyke . . . What are we going to do . . . ?!

SANDY Fuck you! You used my clients' money to cover your fucking movie stars' losses. My people whose lives you've trashed—working and saving and living only to find that at the end of the American rainbow—there's you.

BURT What are we going to do?

SANDY *(contempt)* What're we gonna do? I'm going to pay them back. If I were you, there is only one thing I would do. I would kill myself. That's what I would do. I mean, think about it. Think about it. *(beat)* It's the only decent thing left.

Sandy exits. There is a long moment. Burt goes upstage to a desk and takes out an automatic pistol. He blows the back of his head off. There is red blood pooling everywhere. Then silence. Then someone starts to slowly come down the spiral staircase. Before we see who it is, the stage darkens.

Blackout

SCENE TWO

ANTON KILGALLEN, *a gentleman in his late sixties—early seventies, sits in a sleek modernist chair with a cup of tea and a saucer balanced neatly on his knees. There is a Japanese screen behind him. Cranes and whatnot. Waitstaff prepare tables upstage. A sense that this is a restaurant before opening.*

ANTON   Later that day—for it was already past midnight—the man who walked out of that room got on a plane and left the country for what was to have been a quick fiduciary recovery mission. A year later, he has yet to return to his family and to his home.

Everyone knows about Burt Sarris, and how he died by his own hand, and what he stole, and all that. But very few know, or even heard of Sanford—Sandy—Sonnenberg, except that he fairly quickly dropped out of the big gaping maw which we refer to as "news." Yes. My story is of Sandy Sonnenberg. He is my subject. Son of Judah, grandson of Sholem, Isaac, and so on, an ancient family of moneylenders going back hundreds of years to the very beginnings of the eastern European ghettos. The line ends with him. *(leaning towards us, conspiratorial whisper)* And I am going to tell the story as if we were great, good, old friends.

He examines a letter in his hand. It is written on thin airmail stationery in a flowing and elegant cursive.

ANTON *(cont.)*   The letter came recently, and it was one of those letters one imagines . . . late at night, when one can not sleep, a letter from someone who has caused a great deal of pain. *(beat)* It is, at its simplest, an apology. But not addressed to me. I am owed nothing. I am merely . . . the messenger. But I get ahead of myself. You don't even know me, so let's—just—tell you a bit about myself—my name is Anton Kilgallen. I was born in Baltimore in nineteen—in the thirties, I studied at the Art Institute of Chicago, then went out to Hollywood and worked in the costume department at Metro-Goldwyn-Mayer, where I was in charge of brocade and frogging. Then in the late forties, after a barely salvaged honorable discharge from the Army for— what else—homosexuality, I moved back East to Manhattan in the late forties and worked at a magazine called *Flair* which was unbearably beautiful and which lasted for barely a moment, but which featured the works of Saul Steinberg, Lucien Freud, the bedrooms of designers Oliver Smith and Edward Wormley, a letter from Jean Cocteau, etc. If ever you wish to understand just what elegance was, just how exquisite taste once was, the degree of sophistication in New York at a certain period—go to an antique book dealer and hunt down copies of *Flair,* and you shall be transported. Another story, that.

In New York at that time, there was no place to eat—you could fuck, and you could drink, but not eat. A very few of us— tried to fix that. I went to work in a bistro, got to know the business and eventually, eventually, opened up my own place, Le Singe D'Or, The Golden Monkey, famous for our marvelous sixties haute cuisine; tarragon cheese soufflés, coq au vin, delicate little lamb curries with a yogurt chutney, and lots of artists, Bohemians, Bohemians, Bohemians.

It was nirvana. Insomuch as—well—if your idea of nirvana was a dark little room in the West Fifties filled with writers and artists . . . Le Singe was your place. And so Le Singe became a place not just to eat and drink, but for people of a certain type to congregate, to lounge about, and to laugh. *(beat)* After Le Singe folded in 1976, folded up like a little origami swan napkin, Katie Arlen took me in at her restaurant, Brasserie Arlen. At Le Singe, she had worked for me. A delicate, fragile, brilliant, and strong woman, she had with her infant son, Sam, fled a ghastly early marriage to a pinched and joyless vice principal—she had fled and thrived. Sandy Sonnenberg was her second husband. They were married for twenty-two years. He had made a very safe world for her and for Sam. I introduced them. It was I. I introduced my two best friends. *(beat)* This is a long time ago. I worked for her for a dozen years, eventually became an investor, a partner when we moved to our final location—I put my life savings into the place, and it seemed safe enough, there was a solid and loyal clientele and a bottom line. *(beat)* I lost my life savings in the debacle. By the time it was done. Today I have nothing. Social security. And I am working for someone else's restaurant in the theatre district, doing matinee lunches. Show people know me, they come in for me. And some rather forgettable chicken à la king, which is another story. Let me take you back a bit.

SCENE THREE

Lights up on a large table at Brasserie Arlen. SAM ARLEN—a handsome, scruffy, tattooed young man—Sandy, KATIE ARLEN, Burt, many bottles of wine and plates of charcuterie. Anton joins the table.

ANTON Brasserie Arlen was where we would all catch up. We would dine together late at night on Mondays, after the place had closed, and whoever could come—was welcome. Burt Sarris included. He was working for First Boston when we met. And I began to invite him to join us. This was perhaps our third or fourth dinner with Burt, and Sandy was quite relaxed around him. It was April 1998. We had been watching the wooze-fest in Washington.

SANDY He had a weakness. Which was exploited by unscrupulous people; yes. But. *Acting* on those appetites made him terribly vulnerable, and therefore made *us* less safe.

SAM So you're saying . . . ? He has no right to what? To human—?

SANDY *(over Sam)* Look at the cost! Look at what it has cost!

KATIE No, Sandy! It seems to me that this is the language of *shame;* you get taught to deny your basic appetites, as though desire were filthy.

SANDY But. The President does not have the luxury. Did he? Of indulging?

BURT Sandy is right. He gave his enemies an opening. He made us vulnerable.

8

KATIE If only he had said, "Yes, I did this thing, I am human, I am human, now leave me alone. You puritanical, witch-hunting psychosexual hysterics, can we shut up now . . . and get on with trying to make America actually *better*?" I mean, better . . .

ANTON Yes. "Can we please get on with *real life*? . . ."

SAM Sandy, don't get distracted by Judeo-Christian bullshit. Does anybody think that this country is actually functioning, working? You know, where I teach, what I see in the school, these kids. *That's* the issue. This is the only issue: the horrible inequities. The abandonment of basically sacred duties—and that the political class is just, you know, bizarrely fixated on this blow job and nobody is saying—

KATIE *(taking over from Sam)* Nobody is saying . . . "You life-denying, sexless Cotton Mathers, you joyless Washingtonian *hypocrites*. Get over it!"

ANTON Right! He should have stood up on the desk in the Oval Office and declared, "Hey, I like *pussy* and I like *watermelon,* so sue me!"

BURT *(laughing)* You think those are the exact words he should have used?

SANDY What he did to his family! Unforgivable. That kind of lying, the humiliation. No. He wanted to get caught. *"Please take me down—I am a fraud."*

SAM Hey, look, once they start, this sick, moral policing, I know, in my queer heart, I *know* they're gonna come after us too sooner or later.

KATIE Well. It makes me want to leave the country. Close up this restaurant, head for Barcelona.

SANDY *(ruefully)* No, Katie: Your country is Manhattan. *(He kisses Katie.)* You're safe here.

KATIE *(shaking her head)*   This doesn't feel like the age of safety. Everything in this city—has changed—sex, food. Food—my God, how it has changed! Power—it's all so much bigger or deadlier . . . When did the stakes get so high? I'll tell you: when cafeterias went out of style.

BURT   Well. To me, right now, in here, it feels pretty safe, and the food—hey; if one's home were actually the most comforting place in the world, this is what dinner there would taste like. How do you do it?

KATIE   Butter. Lots of butter.

BURT   Sandy, why didn't you ever join any of the big houses, say, Goldman? Tens of billions for you to play with there.

SANDY   My father started the firm, and I like to keep it personal. The old New York. The New York of recognition. So many things get swallowed up and homogenized today. How many times has your bank changed names? Half a dozen? And who owns it? Nobody. So, I stayed put. You like working for a big firm?

BURT   Actually, it gives me a certain power, but I'm not going to do this forever. I have ambitions that go beyond making money for people. That have to do with philanthropy, righting wrongs, maybe a sort of modified, postmodern Robin Hood business.

SAM   You mean actually stealing from the rich to give to the poor? Cool, a Marxist money manager; now I've seen it all.

BURT   No, I'm a full-blown ravenous capitalist, but, I think— given my world—these rich people, my Hollywood clients, and their big paydays, their disease of fame and special treatment . . . No. I don't want to live in that sea for my whole little fish life. *(beat)* I mean, come on, come on, tell me this; Sandy, let me ask you. Taking care of these clients? Does that do it for you?

Sandy grins. He shakes his head.

KATIE *(laughing)*   Yeah, Sandy, does that do it for you? Come on baby, answer . . .

SANDY   Please.

ANTON   This is a very important question!

SANDY *(after a moment of careful thought, watched by all)*   Hey. I would have to be an exceptionally shallow man at my age, at this point in my life, to answer "yes" to that question. There's the internal stuff.

SAM *(surprised)*   What kind of internal stuff? You have internal stuff? Sandy!

SANDY *(shaking his head)*   Sam, you're so young, you think the heart just dies when you turn thirty. Watch; you'll see, and you'll be so shocked at how *small* a sixty-year-old man can feel. There are days when I feel like a child.

Katie kisses him; he holds her hand.

SAM *(laughing)*   You have nightmares? Master of the Universe Sandy Sonnenberg? I never thought . . .

SANDY *(laughing)*   They are not to be talked about. Too dangerous to tempt the fates. Of course I have nightmares! I can't list the things I'm afraid of, it would go on for days.

SAM *(grinning)*   You mean you feel pain, just like other people? You cry and quake? Like me? That *can't* be true!

SANDY *(to Burt)*   Sam just had his heart broken. He thinks he's the first . . .

SAM *(laughing; a wide grin)*   It's true. I'm bleeding here. I am. And nobody has ever suffered the way I'm suffering right now!

SANDY   I'm telling you, my darling, if you insist on dating Australian surfers named *Christian,* then, like all hypercaffeinated, overly articulate little Jewish boys of Manhattan, you will get your heart handed to you, like a soggy knish.

11

ANTON   And how would *you* know, Sandy?

There is laughter. He shakes his head.

SANDY   I'm very happy here tonight. *(Beat. More soberly)* Anyway, Burt, no, I don't intend to die in regret like some Dickensian bookkeeper. Maybe I just want to sit around, get underfoot, and stare at my gorgeous goddamn wife and get monstrously fat on her cooking. Maybe I'll come work here. That would be nice. To be alongside my wife all day. Make love to her in the cold storage locker in mid-July.

KATIE   *(surprised, delighted)*   Wow. Let me kiss you, Sandy Sonnenberg—my plan is working.

SANDY   You have a plan? What is it?

KATIE   I'm not about to share that with you after all this time, but it involves defrosting.

SANDY   *(a toast)*   To thawing out, then.

They kiss. There is a moment.

ANTON   *(to us)*   Later on that night, the talk was of the danger of having too much good fortune. And I remember, everyone admitted to having a voice in the back of their heads, warning something. . . .

SAM   The schoolteacher who got shot for his ATM card. I knew him; I had met him. It rattled all of us, all of us who went into it, sort of "We're gonna change everything" . . .

BURT   You teach in Bushwick, right? Dude—that's like guns, knives, seventy percent dropout rate, you put yourself in harm's way. Why?

Sam shrugs.

KATIE   I've asked him to come work here with me. He's the best pastry chef I know.

Sam stands.

SAM But *that* won't do it. There's something about the little world we inhabit, these dinners, all this, it won't do it, it won't protect us—and besides, I don't want to spend my life pioneering new uses of the pomegranate.

SANDY What Sam is doing is terrific. My God. *Anybody* can do what I do and what Burt does. Hell: You can train a *seal* to make money.

SAM *(another shrug)* Yeah, so, I guess it's up to me then, just keepin' it real in the New York public school system.

BURT *(mid-thought)* —I guess we're all saying the same thing—I get scared that everything can be taken away as easily as it was given. I'm very superstitious. The gods need their sacrificial lambs.

SAM Oh, they have them; and let me tell you—they're not white. *(beat)* I took my kids to the Temple of Dendur last week.

KATIE I used to sit there with you for hours when you were a kid. And did they love it?

SAM To them the most magical place of my childhood meant not a thing. All that registered is that the access afforded by this trip to this ancient thing reconstructed in this gorgeous glass building is how *little* access they have. Most of them don't even have textbooks to learn what the Temple of Dendur means.

There is a moment.

SANDY Textbooks can be purchased, Sam.

SAM *(stunned)* Sandy. Are you serious? My understanding was that for you philanthropy—would come later. Your third act.

SANDY Maybe this is it. Maybe this is Act Three—my third act. *(a shrug)*

SAM *(touched, surprised)*   They need scholarships. Scholarships to whatever higher education they can attain. Be it Harvard, MIT, or Brooklyn College.

BURT   The Sonnenberg Fund for Education.

SANDY   So be it.

Sandy raises his glass. Sam laughs, delighted. They drink. There is a moment.

BURT *(quietly)*   Last year I was lucky enough to take on this movie star—the guy has four slots a year, each worth ten mil, so I got him to donate five percent off the top of each slot to—this great AIDS hospice, and this little broke outfit is suddenly—sitting there with a two million bucks—and of course my movie star has a tax break which means that none of this cost him one precious little dime.

KATE   Who is it? Who is it? Who is it?

BURT   I'm sworn to secrecy.

ANTON *(to us, as lights fade on the restaurant)*   And the night went on, very late, dreams and biographies and stories we'd heard before, and it gave me pleasure to see Burt fitting in. Because I had taken a liking to him, a paternal liking, and I knew he was very lonely. Though very public, with lots of friends. He seemed more fragile to me than he let on.

But things had been very good for him and he did have a marvelous roster of young Hollywood names and soon he left First Boston, and set up his own little boutique. And like a talisman, bestowing upon its owner unarguable taste, insight, and gravitas, was his growing association with Sanford Sonnenberg. *(beat)* So now. A late lunch in a Tribeca restaurant—two old friends, Sandy and I. A few weeks after the dinner . . .

Scene Four

The lights shift. A small restaurant in Tribeca. The room is pale yellow, has a magnificent flower arrangement in the center. Sandy has a large bourbon before him, and is idly stirring the ice.

ANTON You are the only man I know who still drinks bourbon at lunch. It's so fifties.

SANDY Bourbon stills my nerves better than anything I've ever found—oh, and while we're on the subject—I brought back quaaludes for you from Zurich.

ANTON My last vice—thank God for the Swiss and their passion for pharmaceuticals and thank you—

SANDY No, I like it, I like breaking the law a little bit—it's good for me. So tell me something, Anton, I just, I'm curious. How do you know Burt?

ANTON I think it was at Pat Buckley's . . .

SANDY *(a sigh)* Of course it was.

ANTON . . . or no. No. He is a friend of the daughter of Brooke Hayward, Marin Hopper, that's right, there was a dinner and he was—

SANDY *(cuts him off)* Are you fucking him?

ANTON What makes you think that?

SANDY Well. I assume he's gay.

ANTON I actually must say I don't think so.

SANDY What do you mean?

ANTON By the by not that I'm offended but . . . . I am perfectly capable . . . Sandy, of friendships with younger men that do not involve sex, or money, or sex and money, actually.

SANDY Are you saying he's straight?

ANTON Why are you asking?

SANDY Should we have a wine?

ANTON A Lafite?

SANDY A Lafite? What's the occasion?

ANTON We don't see one another much anymore.

SANDY What, aside from every Monday?

ANTON I mean alone.

SANDY A Lafite it is. A nice '86. *(studying the menu)* I like him. The Dover sole?

ANTON For me, the John Dory.

SANDY How long have you known him?

ANTON A few years. He's doing quite well.

SANDY Clients?

ANTON Movie people, show people, music types, art types, gallery owners, and I think a parrot.

SANDY The parrot is a client?

ANTON A pet, a large revolting and bitchy mauve bird. Very possessive of him too.

SANDY This is not a heterosexual; straight people do not have parrots.

ANTON Why don't you give me a list of what straight people have and do not have.

SANDY Do you think he's attractive?

ANTON Do you, Sandy?

SANDY Do you want some artichokes or something?

ANTON You're attracted to him.

SANDY   You make everything about sex.

ANTON   I don't make everything about sex. I don't have to. Everything *is* about sex.

SANDY   It's so irksome that you assume that my only interest in someone might be sexual.

ANTON   The tuna tartare is supposed to be very nice here.

SANDY   He's done well; I've done a bit of research. I am thinking of untethering myself a bit—I'm too tightly wound.

ANTON   Retiring? You?

SANDY   *(tries to hold back his tears, successfully)*   I'm so fucking sad all the time, I don't know why. These suits I wear, they make me sad. Katie doesn't make me sad, but she loves me so much—that saddens me, because I realize my feelings are so—there are many channels within cauterized and I want to do something. One more day of watching money flow like water and I'll go mad. *(wipes his eyes)*

ANTON   Sandy. My darling.

Anton holds his friend's hand. Sandy laughs.

SANDY   I manage about four hundred million dollars in investments for my clients and have to find a way to retire that they could accept. And that acceptance will be a lot easier if I find someone who will make them more money than I do, and that's Burt. Every night I go to bed with these numbers in my head. Names and Numbers. The Sauls, the Burmans, the Metzkers, the Cohns, the Rands, the Orrs, the Meyersons. . . . these staunch old-world Jews . . . *(He is nearly hysterical, grief stricken.)*—the Golds, whose parents were . . . served by my father. And nobody ever asked me, did they? The assumption was . . . *(Sandy laughs.)* I have to stop crying, don't I? *(beat)* Something about Burt got to me. I need to do my due diligence so I'm asking you . . .

ANTON I had no idea. Have you talked to Katie?

SANDY She would be thrilled to see me retire. I'm having a meeting with Burt tomorrow. *(He stops.)* I have no idea what's wrong with me.

ANTON I do: You're gay.

SANDY Jesus, not this again—don't you ever get tired of living your life so utterly—prescribed—within the narrow confines of a sexual identity?

ANTON I am not the one who contorted himself hither and yon for the sake of a kind of . . . bastardized assimilation, Sanford. I have done as I've pleased, whereas it is quite clear to me that you, my dear, have not.

SANDY You understand nothing of how I live. Fuck this coyness: You're an observer, a bystander.

ANTON I understand perfectly. We've had these lunches before. There was the assistant curator at the Whitney; Julian whatever his-name from Coos Bay, Oregon; there was the marvelous wine salesman from Wainscott; there was the execrable trust-fund poet who lived on St. Barts . . . and not that you ever—God forbid acted on it—except for the one time with me—

SANDY Please. The one time, which you never—

ANTON But God, you—endlessly parade your schoolgirl crushes, and I frankly find it rather—Look, why don't you just fuck him and get it out of your system! *(Beat. He stops, shocked at his own vitriol.)* We're both overwrought; I don't know why. Here you are, trying to be honest with me about your life. As best you're able to.

SANDY You think I've wasted my life. I love Katie so much. I get separation anxiety if I'm away from her for too long and yet I love being away from her. I crave it, and then if we're apart, I go crazy. I have no—my gyroscope is fucked up, I think. My gyroscope is—I bonded myself to this woman, this perfection. Sometimes—we have—we might go through a period where for reasons of exhaustion or age or something, schedule, we don't make love for a bit, very little touching goes on, and I think, "One day we'll both be dead, I've got to make love to her because one day I won't be able to . . ." *(He starts to cry again.)* I love her so much that it makes me hate her. I think I might be having a breakdown, is that possible?

ANTON   You're simply too old to bottle things up anymore, kitty cat.

SANDY   Oh, I see. Is that it?

ANTON   Let's have some wine. Where's the wine?

He whispers to a waiter standing in the background. There is a moment. Sandy composes himself. The wine is poured. There is silence. Sandy shakes his head.

ANTON *(cont.)*   This is just a bad day.

SANDY   Do you discuss this with Katie ever? Our shared history?

ANTON   That we had an affair in 1962? Please? It's a joke, it's an actual joke, really, and an old one. Why do you ask?

SANDY   Oh come on—it was not an affair, it was too brief to be an affair, it was somewhere in the vicinity of a minor blip on the Kinsey scale.

ANTON   So to speak.

SANDY   Of course, it was fun. But infantile.

ANTON   I think yes, infantile, our little dalliance was utterly childish, yes.

SANDY Burt flirted with me. That evening, it was flirting. I recognize flirtation. I know it, I understand it when I see it.

ANTON Yeah. Well. So what? People flirt. Seducers flirt. He might well have been, yes. He does that, Sandy, it means very little, some people are flirts, it's their mode. *(beat)* But what you're saying is, yes, you DO find him attractive. *(beat)* Let me ask you a question: Do you not regret the choice you made, Sandy?

SANDY Never. That doesn't mean it wasn't hard. That it did not require rigor, expunging . . . self-denial.

ANTON Yes, it must be hard to kill a part of yourself.

SANDY Which part? The sensualist? The bitch within? Please? No. Do you ever regret the choice you made, Anton? You've lived through your friends, all your best friends. Haven't you. And sex? Hustlers, and boyfriends now and then, with whom the sex life lifts, and then sinks. And us friends. Christmas with us. Or the Buckleys or Kitty Hart, or the . . . whomevers. What have you got aside from that? *(beat)* No, I don't regret my "choice," as you put it. You've never had love, have you? You've had facsimiles and replicas, but all the aloneness has gone unabated no matter how many friends you collect; you are a curiosity, and an extra man . . . alone. This life of yours does not work—we're not allowed to say that anymore but we all know it.

ANTON Do we?

SANDY Look at Sam. God knows, he goes to clubs, he's like voracious, it's boys and new boys . . .

ANTON Perhaps, but I would say that at the moment, old friend, I am not the one who feels alone. I am not the one whose life isn't working. Have I missed anything? I've had loads of sex, boatloads of lovers, been entertained, have a little pin money, and so on. What else is there?

SANDY A structure to life, a family! A family! You're dying of loneliness.

ANTON Only on Sundays. Listen to yourself: "structure, rigor, expunging, self-denial"—listen to yourself! All those years of therapy, all those years of inculcation, and really, all you've got is what you were force-fed by some ghastly psychiatrist from the Eisenhower days! I wish he could see you now. I would love to show them: "Here he is—your star patient—your prize pupil, adapted and well-adjusted and spinning off into chaos."

SANDY I never said my life was simple. Dr. Schiffman told me how hard it would be. There were no lies. *(furious, frustrated, choked)* Jesus, Anton, this is fucking Greek to you, isn't it? Sometimes I wonder if we're even still friends!

ANTON *(to us)* We ate. He drank a bit more than one might usually expect. There were no more tears, but I was shaken, I must admit. It was a violent and hostile encounter, and so my old turbulent friend Sandy Sonnenberg, faltering, second-guessing, lurching through some very private dream, around the time of our lunch, went on to disastrously forge a relationship with Burt Sarris. My fault, I suppose. *(beat; scornfully)* "Fault." God. *(beat)* We never imagine what's to come—do we?—when we first see someone we *must* know . . . the frisson that first runs through you. A young man walks into your restaurant—you can tell he's very clever, and you can tell he's alive and that he's suffering in that particular way that so excites you. Forty years before that lunch in Tribeca, when Tribeca was still a place of spice warehouses and cobblestones. Forty years ago, Sandy had wandered into Le Singe and held court in a corner, expounding on everything from Leonard Bernstein to Sputnik to Yves Klein and JFK. I knew right away: Sandy Sonnenberg was simply someone I had to get to know.

Lights fade on the two men.

The Goldberg Variations *continues from a record player in the West Village apartment of Anton Kilgallen. Furnished in "Robsjohn-Gibbings, junk shoppe classicism, and Third Avenue Dada," (to quote an article on the period from* Flair *magazine). It is night, and it is snowing, which we see through the large plate glass window overlooking Abingdon Square.* YOUNG ANTON *and* YOUNG SANDY *have just come in from the snow, are discarding coats. Anton is smoking, putting Bach on the record player. One entire wall is covered with framed artwork from* Flair, *forming a sort of collage. There is Saul Steinberg, Cocteau, Lucien Freud, Tamayo, and so on, some of it original cover art.*

SANDY   But finally, I guess I think the whole movie was messier than he was. What did you think, Anton?

ANTON   Well, I don't know, I love Monty Clift, he's great, and tortured, God knows, if you knew him, Sandy . . . really tortured—but I'm not really quite sure he's Sigmund fucking Freud. And I think John Huston wasn't either. And P.S.: The clothes were wrong.

SANDY   I love Freud, he was just such a great writer. He had such clarity and specificity and . . . heart. Compassion.

ANTON   I know, but his followers, oh my, well, perhaps not so imaginative as the master.

SANDY   I think it's also that he appeals to my Viennese side—my dad was born there. So—you've been to a psychiatrist?

ANTON   It's rather like crabs—you get bit, you scratch, and then you apply something nasty and try never to let it happen again. It was required of me, a problem in the Army.

SANDY   Really? Jeez. What was the problem?

ANTON   The Army? Please. It's all men. Sweat. Underwear, showers, teen yearning. The Army. I mean, what did they think was going to happen? They booted me very quickly, I was relieved—it freed me to come to New York . . . *(after a moment)* In any event, I suspect even then I knew more than those squeamish goddamn Army shrinks. About everything happening here. *(He taps his heart.)* And who cares about what happens here? *(taps his head)*

SANDY   Then you're a very damn lucky man, Anton.

ANTON   That, Sandy, is quite true. *(He looks out the window and sighs.)* The first snowfall of the winter. I always love that moment in this city.

He brushes snow off both of their coats. His hand lingers on Sandy's shoulder for a moment before Sandy gracefully pulls away.

SANDY   Me too—I know—because you've come through that big stretch between . . .

ANTON *(at the drinks tray)*   Bourbon . . . right? Rocks?

SANDY   Yeah, please.

ANTON   What exactly do you mean by "big stretch"?

SANDY   From February or March, which was usually the last time it snowed.

ANTON   Of course. Right.

SANDY   I'm a winter person. The world, I think is divided into two kinds of people: summers and winters.

ANTON   As good a delineation as any other, I guess. Though I'm more of an autumnal—

SANDY *(over him)*   My family, for instance, abandons the city in late May, and I have the place entirely to myself—until the week after Labor Day. And I realized that none of the pleasures of the beach: lemonade and boats—they're in Quoque—under a blinding sun—they have this ridiculous white house and it—

(Beat. He drinks some more. He is very nervous.) I have no idea what I am saying.

ANTON Nor do I. Not to worry—you had moved into your dislike of summer . . .

SANDY Too lit. Too much daylight. Depressing.

ANTON The summer can be.

SANDY Ugh. All that—leisure and heat; the only good part is having the city somewhat to myself. I get so exhilarated when it snows and everything is new. Think about it? The first snow of the season: It's a perfect marker.

ANTON *(remembering, nodding)* I think I know what you mean . . .

SANDY I always think about what's come between. Then and now. That you're a different person now. The last time it snowed, you ask yourself "Where were you?" "Where was I?"

ANTON I was at the restaurant, trying to finish it . . . We opened in a blizzard, I lit the fireplace in the back, where you like to sit, and nobody came in, for two whole days, not even my friends, and then suddenly . . . it was a party.

SANDY I was at school. My last winter in Princeton, and I was so damn sad about it. I loved it there, the little town, I had some friends who were very down on it, down on the whole uptight buttoned-down aspects of the place, which sure, yes, it's a little . . . tightly wrapped. But less tightly wrapped than the world I come from, which—*(beat)* I keep talking about my family. I really have to stop.

ANTON No, actually, you can talk about anything you like.

SANDY The thing is this: We're in a series of wars, my father and I. Anton, you see: I want to join the Peace Corps. He didn't even vote for Kennedy; he's so assimilated, so country club . . . I heard Kennedy's speech about the Peace Corps, and I thought, "I want to serve, I want to help."

ANTON   And you're being dissuaded?

SANDY   To put it mildly. I am expected to go into the family
business; I am the only son. It's money, the business—they fiddle
with money, clean it up, polish it, make more of it, magic tricks
and sleight of hand and late night phone calls.

ANTON   Sounds like medicine.

SANDY   It is. Emergencies, flights to Europe, somber joyless
meetings. And dull people.

ANTON   So what? I left home and never looked back. You're
twenty-one, Sandy, and you should do what you want, my
friend. It's not worth it, trying to please. It is a fucking fool's
errand.

SANDY   Right.

*There is a moment. Anton is very close to Sandy, who finally darts
away.*

SANDY *(cont.)*   Anyway, in Princeton, the last time it snowed I
went for a walk and I thought, "Where will I be when it snows
again?" I cried, because I'd had such a good four years. I was
just, I wandered around the campus for hours, I had this
cashmere overcoat on, and it was totally soaked . . .

ANTON   And here you are. Eight months later.

Anton touches Sandy's cheek. Sandy nervously moves away.

SANDY   I love staying up all night. I do, it's my favorite thing, I
don't like to sleep. I have never been able to sleep.

ANTON   New York was not intended for sleep. If you want to
sleep, move to Baltimore.

SANDY   No. I never wanted to live anywhere else, I never will,
I'm a New Yorker . . . *(looking around)* I like your place. It's very
Bohemian. Very hectic.

ANTON Hectic—God, I've never heard *that* before. Is that bad?

SANDY No, it's unrestrained. Your friends, the people I've been meeting—so much energy unfettered, so little kept inside, you do whatever you like—well, you should see my parents' house, I mean, you know, it's all Duncan Phyfe stuff, you can't really ever quite relax. You can't . . . What's that? What's *Flair* . . . ?

Sandy points to the Flair *magazine art.*

ANTON A magazine which was published for a very short time, twelve issues only. I worked there, I made myself over there, after Bendel's . . . I worked there when I was kicked out of the Army.

SANDY I remember seeing them when I was a kid.

ANTON It was fun—it folded. Too expensive; rather ahead of its time. The cover always had a hole in it, revealing some bit of art underneath. Something hidden peeking out. One day I'll show it to you. But right now I'm sorry to say, I really, really only want to kiss you.

SANDY *(not looking at Anton)* I know.

ANTON May I, do you think?

Sandy stands by the window, looking out. He shakes his head no.

SANDY I mean I don't know.

ANTON You've never done this, have you? You waited until you graduated, right? You couldn't bear to confuse yourself any more while you were at school, so you waited until . . .

SANDY Right. I mean, tenth grade, this boy and I jacked off together and I . . . He never wanted to talk about it, and then, nor did I.

ANTON Sandy, I am, by nature, a deferential man, and so I shan't pursue this.

SANDY *(disappointed)*   Oh. Okay. Really?

ANTON *(laughing)*   Too much. Don't look so disappointed. I mean, you're gorgeous and tortured and Jewish, and terribly unsure of yourself in a cocksure sort of way, which I adore, but I'm not going to take you. I'm not built for that.

SANDY *(bellicose)*   I'm not—what does my being Jewish have to do with anything? And I don't think I'm cocksure, at all, whatever that means, at all, I just . . .

ANTON *(smiling)*   You what? You've been coming into my restaurant, kitty cat, staring at me for a week. Sitting alone at a table reading fucking Genet? And Proust, no less, sitting around, lounging with a martini and a pack of Gauloises, making notes in the margins, with a big fucking fountain pen, which incidentally stained my nice linen tablecloth, batting your eyes at me like we're at the Princeton library.

SANDY   Yeah, well. You looked happy. Like someone having fun. It's sort of contagious; I thought I might catch it.

ANTON   Well, God knows, one wouldn't want that. I mean, you might die.

SANDY   I'm really sorry about the tablecloth.

Sandy kisses Anton. His hands explore Anton's body. He pushes Anton back into the wall, kissing him the whole time.

ANTON   Right. I don't think I can forgive you; they're very expensive and—Are you all right, I don't want to—

SANDY   No. I'm not, I'm . . . *(kissing him; shuts Anton up)* I'm on the verge of detonating. I've wanted to do that for years—and in October, during the missile crisis, when I thought the whole world was about to explode, I thought I'd have died without ever—

ANTON   Look. Wait. This is my hand. I want you to hold it. Feel it. Okay? Take your time. My hand. You want to know me? Look at me. Look.

He kisses Sandy again, and removes his jacket, unbuttons his shirt, and kisses Sandy's stomach.

ANTON *(cont.)*   It's good to know who you're touching, and what it feels like; last time it snowed you were one person, now you're another, okay?

SANDY   What's going to happen to me?

ANTON   Nobody knows the answer to that question. It's pointless. Look at me. It's pointless.

Sandy kisses Anton hungrily, voraciously. The lights fade down, with both men undressing in the near dark, lit mostly by the snow, which is illuminated by the streetlight outside the window.

OLDER ANTON   Four months. It lasted. Just four. November 1962. February 1963. Some of the things we did: Andy Warhol had his first solo show. I took him. We kissed, and drank bad wine, and loved the pictures. We saw *Dr. No* and *Lolita* together. On the same fucking day! We held hands and smoked in the movie theatre. To this day, I avoid the Beekman Cinema, as we had our hands down each other's fronts for the entire film and left dazed and sticky. And that was just *Dr. No;* I can't even talk about *Lolita.* Went downtown. Drank at the Ninth Circle, danced in the back room, stayed out all night. He had a car, and we would drive around the city in it; you still could, then. People who are lost in love own Manhattan, or they used to; not sure it has the same effect now that it is in color. So to speak—it was such a short time—it was—brief—and he—was in—in love and I believe—he was also in hell.

SCENE SIX
FEBRUARY 1963

The office of DR. MORITZ SCHIFFMAN, *Carnegie Hill. Late afternoon, milky wintery light filters in to the basement office. The only sound is from a Nelson sunburst clock. CLICK. CLICK. CLICK. Sandy is seated on an Eames sofa across from Dr. Schiffman, who is sitting on an Eames chair, his feet up on its ottoman. There are several cacti in the room.*

SANDY   —I don't know, all I can say is, I don't—I'm at sea, it's—!

SCHIFFMAN   Well, it's best if you simply start at the beginning, Mr. Sonnenberg. It's all right. We have time.

SANDY   I read this article about you, about how you have been able to help homosexuals . . . Is it true?

SCHIFFMAN   Yes. Yes. It is. *(beat; gently, paternal)* If a person who has an affinity for same-sex sex wishes to be helped in a move to a heterosexual life, he can be.

SANDY   He can be. But . . . ?

SCHIFFMAN   Yes. There is a "but." You are obviously very bright, which helps. I find the more . . . ready-witted the subject, the more open to the light they are. It's very hard. It's a torturous battle. It takes a brave soul. I've been able to help many young men. I think we have to see. We have to see. If we can relate to each other. Yes?

There is silence.

SANDY   How does it work?

Schiffman stares at the jittery young man, who is looking around the room. Schiffman gently continues.

SCHIFFMAN   The homosexual patient is in a terrible fix, Mr. Sonnenberg. He derives pleasure, physical pleasure from that which is most harmful. Therefore the incentive to

29

change relies upon an actual understanding of the pleasure/pain principle, about which more later, but—he can be aided.

SANDY Well, no, I read about that—You have to—redefine your idea of pleasure—

SCHIFFMAN Refocus it. I think. Yes. The yearning to change is perhaps the most salient ingredient to this equation. It is possible, if you want it. Do you want to change?

SANDY *(a rush of words)* Look, I opened a door, you know, somehow, and I don't know what it is, it's just awful. I don't know how to close it.

SCHIFFMAN Yes, exactly, well put, Mr. Sonnenberg.

SANDY A sentence, a curse. It's awful.

SCHIFFMAN Many people use exactly the same words, Mr. Sonnenberg. I know what this feels like for you, I think. Our sexuality is so vital to us, to what makes us human, and it can cause so much agony. I think your pain is a very good thing. It is telling us that you know what to do.

SANDY Yes. I just—think of that life, and what it amounts to. The people who—so sad, it makes me so sad. My stomach just—it just . . . *(Beat. He thinks.)* I went through—I had one experience in summer camp, with a boy who played tennis, he was coaching me in tennis and he—

SCHIFFMAN May I ask? This is—perhaps—an older boy?

SANDY Yes, and he was athletic and masculine and, anyway, it always stayed with me and now I just want to get on . . .

SCHIFFMAN You're very brave. Obviously in a great deal of pain. I want you to describe this experience. Just let yourself drift back to that time. Try.

There is silence again. Sandy lights a cigarette, as does Dr. Schiffman.

SANDY   Nobody was around, it was late in the afternoon, in the middle of summer, excruciatingly hot, and wet.

SCHIFFMAN   I understand.

SANDY   Humid. Torpid. And after we had played tennis for three hours, everyone else was at the lake and we were exhausted and I had strained or cramped a muscle in my leg, my upper thigh . . .

SCHIFFMAN   Yes.

SANDY   And he said he could help; it really hurt quite a bit.

SCHIFFMAN   Yes.

SANDY   And we went into the shed where the equipment was and he asked me to lay down on the bench, and I think I knew but I didn't know, at the same time, and I had my shirt off, so did he, because they had stuck to the skin, it was the humidity . . . *(beat)* So I had my shorts on, and he started massaging my leg, and then it got closer to my thigh, the inner thigh, right? And I just could feel myself being aroused. It was very silent. It was totally quiet. Except for both of us gulping occasionally, and his hands moved down my thighs, he could see I had an erection, and his—his hand brushed against it over my shorts and I moaned, I just moaned, I was so hard. I just, I loved it. He had such strong hands. And then I felt him gently unbuttoning my tennis shorts, my eyes were closed, you see, and his hand just . . . his mouth was on me. And I reached over and touched him. He was hard too, and he wanted me to—and we exploded. Salt and sweat and . . . *(beat)* Summer camp. I could never go back. This older boy who—

Silence. The late afternoon light is changing to dusk. Schiffman is writing on a yellow pad.

SCHIFFMAN   Older boy? Who? Go on?

SANDY I felt something awful lurching inside me when I came. This new kind of terrible silence. Inside of me. As though the doors to the rest of the world could be slammed shut and if anyone ever knew—it would be the very end of me. To describe it as shame doesn't do it justice, it's so much worse than that. It felt like . . .

SCHIFFMAN Yes?

SANDY I felt like—I'm sure you've read *Crime and Punishment*? I felt exactly like Raskolnikov—

SCHIFFMAN Yes? Raskolnikov was a murderer . . . You felt like a murderer? Who were you murdering by having a sexual experience, Mr. Sonnenberg?

There is silence.

SCHIFFMAN *(cont.)* You said you felt like Raskolnikov. Who did he murder?!

SANDY A pawnbroker and her sister.

SCHIFFMAN Women. Yes, two women. He was a killer of women, and you expressed the association of yourself in this homosexual act as being akin to a killer of women . . . ?

SANDY I've been having sex with this man.

SCHIFFMAN He is a little bit older than you, no?

SANDY He's sophisticated and urbane in a way that—the sex is—I had sex in college with girls, and I felt the way I used to feel at synagogue, this rote, these systems, these numbers, what do they all mean? I have no idea, it was mechanical with the girls, as much so as studying for a bar mitzvah, but when Anton and I are having sex, it feels like—*(beat)* Do you like jazz, Dr. Schiffman?

SCHIFFMAN Sure.

SANDY *(excited)*   Going down to the Village and hearing Mingus or Miles Davis. The joy of not knowing what's coming next. That's how I feel when I'm with him. We stay up all night. New York is—New York is completely new to me. His body. I love it. What he is able to do.

SCHIFFMAN   What exactly is that?

SANDY   I become—I absorb—part of him. I incorporate an enormous and very dangerous exclusive—secret. And the thing is . . . *(He is very upset.)* I don't want it. I don't want any part of it. Whatever that secret is. This ease, the comfort he has—where did it come from? From what? *(silence)* I see these men. His friends. The nightlife, the—refusal to alight. Bars. Passion for these parties, where some men call each other by woman's names, which makes me so—unhappy—and—he doesn't but— they're unhinged, there are no rules. I could be reduced to— *(beat; angry)* I have—I am being watched. My parents are watching me. My father is very powerful.

SCHIFFMAN   Is he? Perhaps that is something we could work on. I think it's important.

SANDY *(upset and excited)*   He exerts tremendous power. Like a— like a government—like a central government very far away, making legislation, and edicts and statutes . . . from afar. I want you to help me.

SCHIFFMAN   Mr. Sonnenberg, I think you can be helped, spectacularly, spectacularly by therapy, by analysis, five days a week . . .

SANDY   I could do that.

SCHIFFMAN   Look. It's a rough road, my boy. And don't think it's easy. Don't fool yourself. You must understand that this is very hard work and takes a long time, and all I ask is—I ask two things—that you forgive yourself—because you're going to slip—it's the rules of the game—you're gonna slip—that's one thing—and the other—is that you try hard to be open with me.

SANDY   I want to. You—I—you're giving me—I feel a little bit less . . .

SCHIFFMAN   Alone? Good. Good. I have so much respect for my patients in your situation. But this struggle is worth it. To have family, children, to continue life—create life—to watch our children grow—to know the love of a woman—these are very holy pursuits, very righteous, and so worthy of your efforts . . .

SANDY *(almost in tears)*   Thank you.

SCHIFFMAN   It is very important to begin considering how you're going to break off your relationship with this man you are seeing.

SANDY   He's my friend.

SCHIFFMAN   Yes, I understand. And let's see if we can redact this into a true friendship—you have more power than you think— but it is important that you begin to consider this withdrawl. You are going to feel terribly alone in this. But you never will be. There will be times when you hate me. I will know. But I will understand. You will miss appointments. I shall charge you but never abandon you. What you are doing takes great courage, and you should know: You will not be alone.

So we have come to the end of our first hour. I'm very glad you've come to me and I believe I can help you. There is hope. There is hope.

Anton appears, turns to us.

ANTON *(reading)*   "The homosexual is imprisoned in a cycle of instant gratification and despair, ever renewing, ever corroding, trapped on a Ferris wheel of hallucinatory pain, joyless pleasure, and ceaseless, aching emptiness . . . *(smiles; a small laugh)* From the collected essays of Doctor Moritz Schiffman.

Of course, in the life of the heart, we know that there are cures and diseases, but sometimes, I have noticed, it is *very* hard to tell which is which.

Blackout

End of Act One

ACT TWO

Le Singe d'Or restaurant, later that night. How to describe the place? The wallpaper is trios of see-no-evil, hear-no-evil, speak-no-evil monkeys in gold; that should say it all. Sandy is with his mother, LILLIAN SONNENBERG, *a sophisticated New Yorker who likes to smoke (cigarette holder) and drink (old-fashioned, extra cherry) and is doing both.*

LILLIAN I'll tell you something, Sandy, having you back in town is really terrific, finally your mother has someone to go to the theatre with, though I have to tell you, I don't understand that play—I mean—are all college professors and their wives—was that what it was like at Princeton—*(She looks around.)* I'd love another drink; what a cute place you took me to, it's so fun, with the crazy monkeys . . .

SANDY My friend owns it.

LILLIAN Well, I like the place, it's fun and . . . gay. *(Sandy nods, weary.)* But I'd love another old-fashioned. *(She gestures to someone—"Could I have another?")* Anyway, was there a son or wasn't there?

SANDY What son where?

LILLIAN The play!

SANDY It was an imaginary son, mother.

LILLIAN Why were they fighting like that? Your father and I have never had—especially in public; sometimes in private we would—well—he can't fight, he's so—he's an iron mountain, the Azenberg, I call him. Which isn't necessarily a reference to our sex life, kiddo. Boy.

Anton comes to the table, bearing a new drink for Mrs. Sonnenberg.

ANTON Here you are, Mrs. Sonnenberg, I saw you needed another . . .

36

SANDY   Mom, this is my friend Anton Kilgallen, he owns the place.

LILLIAN   Oh, it's lovely. Will you sit with us for a moment?

ANTON   In a bit. I have to whip them into shape in the kitchen; there's a problem with the *Boeuf Bourgignon* which needs me, I'm afraid.

He glides off, after grinning at Lillian.

LILLIAN   He has to whip them. Very dashing young man—how do you know him?

SANDY   I come here a bit.

LILLIAN   This is where the arty people go! So much fun; I would love it if you would take me to—I want very much to go to the Village Gate to see Nichols and May, but your father won't go. Do you like Nichols and May?

SANDY   Yes.

LILLIAN *(over him)*   He finally did agree to go see Lenny Bruce once but he sat there like the Azen-Berg, and Lenny got furious at him and directed his entire act to your father who was simply like really—it—it felt like I'd married an Easter Island statue with a yarmulke.

SANDY   Yes, I know that side of him.

LILLIAN   You two! God! My God. Look. Honey. You don't know how to handle him. That's your problem, kiddo.

SANDY   My problem?

LILLIAN *(She looks at the menu.)*   Do you think the *Suprême de Volaille* is good? Ohh—*Rognons de Jeunesse,* can we split—let's split the Moule Marinier, they look good, that Negro couple over there is having them—see, we never go to places like this, my God, do you know how sick I am of l'Pavillon? Every goddamned night with those clients—one of them gave us an oil painting of Golda Meir, a big yellow thing and I'm not hanging it—because pretty she ain't—oh, they have mousse au chocolat for desert and *Oeufs à la Neige*—is that the same as *Ile flottante*?

SANDY I think so.

LILLIAN What are we going to do about you and your father? It's a terrible situation.

SANDY Well, I'll tell you. I refuse to break. I won't give in. Sometimes I think that I should just give in. Come work with him. And then I can't bear the idea.

LILLIAN Good. I don't think you should.

Anton comes over with a tray of little appetizers.

ANTON I thought you might enjoy these *rumaki*. I'll be back in a bit. *(He glides off.)*

LILLIAN I love this place! Where was I? *(She takes a piece of* rumaki *and nibbles it.)*

SANDY You don't want me to go into the business?

LILLIAN Darling, I want you to be happy. I don't care what you do—be happy.

SANDY Lillian, here's the thing. I've gone into psychoanalysis, and I'm doing it five days a week, and I can't pay for it on my allowance.

There is silence. She nods and shrugs finally.

LILLIAN You too, huh? Okay. Well. Without my prying—do you want to talk about it?

SANDY Yeah, maybe in about twenty years. You're so sweet, Mom.

LILLIAN I ain't sweet, Sandy, but—you're the love of my life. There isn't anything I wouldn't do for you. Of course I'll pay for it, but the thing is, what we have to do is to find a way to not let your father know.

SANDY   That would probably be better, I think.

LILLIAN *(laughing)*   You bet your ass, boyo. *(She takes off her earrings and puts them on the table close to Sandy.)* Go to Grossbard and Sons. They'll buy them, no questions asked, tell them you're my son. If they need to call me, give them my private line. That should pay for a year. I'm a very big believer in psychiatry, I really am.

I think it's changed a lot. I had a cousin in Baton Rouge and they gave him shock treatment. And he was such a gentle soul, so delicate, very much like you, and he would have been fine if they just let him be. I was very angry about it. I never knew quite what the problem was, of course. I was much younger than he. But he seemed smart and funny, and sophisticated. He really was so much like you. *(She is staring at Sandy.)*

SANDY   I think I need another drink. What happened to your cousin, Mom?

LILLIAN   Such a nice place. So many men eating here, huh, it's just me and that Negro woman . . . huh. Not a spot for girls?

SANDY   It's still early. What happened to your cousin, Mom?

She lights another cigarette.

LILLIAN   He hanged himself in a boathouse. Not my favorite year, 1933, I moved to New York soon thereafter; you know, I'd just had enough of the incivility and the . . . you know, provincialism. *(beat)* Nothing can be as rough and as savage as the—as the— wall of a family pressing down on someone who just won't conform, so that's why I say to you, if you don't want to come work for Sonnenberg & Sonnenberg, believe me, don't. I've thought about this a great deal. *(Beat. She wipes her eyes.)*

SANDY How do I remind you of your cousin?

LILLIAN *(staring at her son)* He was a sensitive person. He was caring. And tentative. He liked art; he liked to read. He was not like other men. Of course they sent him to a psychiatrist who—I mean—it was very primitive, it was more prison than anything else.

SANDY *(quietly furious)* Do you think I'm not like other men? Do you think I'm strange and delicate, because I'm not.

LILLIAN *(She leans forward.)* Darling. Look. I'm not as worldly as you. I'm a simple gal.

SANDY No you're not.

LILLIAN No, I'm not. And nothing is ever going to happen to you, because you'll always have me. *(She looks around and gasps.)* My God, do you know who just walked in? Truman Capote and James Baldwin! *(beat)* I love being with you, Sandy my dear, it's like a date. I never get to go on dates anymore. The only thing I want in exchange for paying for your psychiatrist is to be able to go out on these dates once a week with you. *(She wipes her eyes, grins, and reaches into her purse and hands Sandy an envelope.)* This is very important, he comes from a long line of people who shun each other, there's a lot of shunning in the Sonnenbergs so—

There's a safe deposit in Lugano with a handful of diamonds, your father gave them to me, and I'm giving them to you—in case anything should happen, they're there for you, they're a life-raft . . . in case you should get shunned, by his side . . .

ANTON *(coming over)* Hi, Mrs. Sonnenberg. I'm going to take your order, are you ready?

LILLIAN You bet.

SANDY I have to . . . uh . . . I have to uh . . . uh . . . excuse me.

LILLIAN *(covered, cheery, debonair)* You bet. I think we start off with the Oysters Rockefeller, another old-fashioned, and . . . go from there? Do you think Mr. Capote would sign my napkin? He's so great!

ANTON   Of course, I'll ask, he's a good friend.

LILLIAN   You have great taste in friends.

Lights fade as Anton takes the order, and exits. Older Anton enters.

ANTON   Yes. "You have great taste," she said, "in friends." And for years I wondered if this was her hardened and manicured way of approving, or at least of—acknowledging me—that I was—who I was—I wondered if she was saying, "I know, and I know, and I know." *(beat)* You know those people who have lives after the mates die? I thought that she would have one of those great third acts. The one where you travel to Turkey and Venice when there is no one there. No. She died first—before the Azenberg—it was a fucking shock. I found it unfair. It made me angry. A broken hip one winter—*too early*—1975—a fall while on a mission—walking her dog, while buying chocolate and cigarettes and vichyssoise on Madison Avenue when it was too cold to go out but staying inside with the Azenberg was driving her mad, followed by pneumonia—She always had a smile for me, and she came into the restaurant a few times and had Welsh rarebit and white asparagus at the bar with me—We never talked about her son.

Scene Two

Anton's apartment, very late at night. Sandy is naked. He lights a cigarette in the dark and then sprays a glass full of seltzer water. He starts to cry. He goes to a cupboard and looks for something—aspirin—and finding the bottle, swallows several with the seltzer.

SANDY   Fuck.

His clothes have been flung about the furniture and he starts to gather them. After a long moment of this Anton comes into the living room, watching silently for a while. He too is naked.

ANTON Sandy.

SANDY It's no good. My head is killing me. I was lying in bed and it was . . .

ANTON Ice helps. I get migraines and lie in the bath with an ice pack over my—

Sandy is shaking his head. He moves away as Anton comes near him.

SANDY *(in agony; getting dressed)* I can't. I can't do it. Whatever it is, I just can't do it. Please, don't talk to me, you speak and I end up back in bed with you. So don't. Don't speak. Please, Anton. I'm not like this. I'm not who you—

ANTON I don't get to speak? That seems unfair.

SANDY No! What do you imagine happening? Us growing old together?

ANTON I hadn't quite gone so far as that, I was . . .

SANDY Where? In what world? Not mine! Passover with the Sonnenbergs and Anton Kilgallen? Of Le Singe d'Or? You coming over to break the fast after—! They—I went to a tail-gate party with an Episcopalian girl once and they—you know, almost had to be sedated . . .

ANTON *(calmly)* I'm very sorry that whatever it is that figures so prominently, call it guilt, in your heart, Sandy, is so immutable. I must confess, it's alien to me. God, you keep coming to me. I don't call you, you keep showing up.

SANDY I know.

ANTON The life I've chosen—is not—I love it. But I had to choose to love it and not fight it. I love sex. I love eating. I love art and fucking and music and talk, Sandy. That's my life. Food and laughing and fucking and romance. It is not a bad life. It is not a bad life. *(beat)* You keep going on and on about what will it be when I'm sixty. I don't know, but if it's anything like the life I have now, I'm sure it'll be terrific. Who knows what will happen? It's 1963, and there are a lot of people like us and every day it gets slightly—I wouldn't say easier, but I was around when they weren't just hunting Reds, they were hunting queers as avidly, just as hungrily. *(beat)* I'm not lonely. You think I can't fall in love? I could fall in love with you if that weren't—so damn fraught.

SANDY *(he has his shirt on, is looking for his coat)*   I can't stand this blur, because it's just sex and then suddenly it's more and the—the—the sex part I could cope with, the compartmentalizing of that would be easy to—but it's suddenly love or something. And I don't want to—I went to a psychiatrist, and he told me the only way is to stop seeing you, is to stop this, is to cauterize this fucking wound of you!

Silence. Anton hands Sandy his coat.

ANTON   You went to a psychiatrist? And he told you to stop seeing me.

SANDY   I'm not a homosexual.

ANTON *(quietly, smiling ruefully)*   Well. I do wish you'd told me that when we were fucking a half hour ago; I hate it when that happens.

SANDY   You can be snide and bitchy, but the fact is, I am not a homosexual, I am not—my doctor, Dr. Schiffman, treats people like me all the time, and he explained it to me, how it works, and I am going to listen to him, I am going to do everything he says.

ANTON   Everything?

SANDY   This is a compulsion, Anton, and if you understood it, this seduction of men very often—very often—is an attempt to avoid being humiliated by them.

ANTON Darling: A question: In our current scenario, I'm a bit confused: Am I tormentor or tormentee? *(beat, as Sandy ties his tie)* You went to Schiffman? You're going to follow his orders to the T? Because he's well-known, this is his shtick, you know.

SANDY Don't. Don't try. And bad-mouth him, he's my only hope. And—it's not just you. It's everything, my mother—my mother relentlessly sexualizing our relationship and smothering me.

ANTON She seemed quite nice at dinner tonight, actually, and very smart. You know, it's one thing to be a happy-go-lucky young queer—we grow old and mellow—but have you ever seen what happens to angry young men as they age . . . ?

SANDY Yes, they grow up and have children, they . . . they grow into men who have families and lives and stability and I don't want to say any more because . . . I want to be your friend, if that's possible.

ANTON Possible? For me or for you? *(beat)* You're already my friend . . . *(He goes toward him, and touches Sandy's hair, and they kiss. Sandy finally pulls away.)* You have so much ahead of you, you could be anything, anyone. The world now is—it's so different—Sandy.

He is tortured. He shrugs. They kiss. Anton tries to take it much further, violently further and very quickly.

SANDY *(also tortured; after going with it, finally pulling away)* I'm sorry, Anton. I can't do this. I love you, I think, but I can't.

ANTON Your problem is not at all sex, Sandy. It is pleasure—it's joy. And that is a much bigger problem. Sex is just parts. I am debauched and I am corrupt, and I am debased, but I don't hurt anyone and I accept it. *(beat)* I hope your psychiatrist is helpful. I'm not sure they've quite fixed the—the—central problem of soothing the unappeasable misery of the joyless, but perhaps they shall. We're still young, and science is moving virtually at the speed of light.

The lights fade as Sandy Sonnenberg gathers his belongings and leaves Anton's apartment. The door slams behind him, and the lights go out.

SCENE THREE
1980

The bar at Brasserie Arlen; Katie, Sandy, and Anton drinking champagne at three in the morning, laughing. They are sharing a bowl of pasta.

KATIE *(laughing, drunk, giddy)* So, Anton, come on, stop hedging, do you think I should marry this man, Anton? I mean, he's your best friend! You introduced us!

ANTON Yes but just—simply as friends! I introduce everyone! I never intended for you two to become paramours—this man? Please. No. Out of the question!

KATIE Well, I mean: What do you think the whole of last year has been? What has the whole of 1980 been?

ANTON A fling.

SANDY *(laughing)* A fling? Are you blind?

ANTON A youthful-not-so-youthful lark. I don't know!

SANDY No. Not at all. It's—it. I—she's not even my type.

KATIE I'm not your type?

SANDY I can't help that we fell in love.

ANTON What is your type?

SANDY I guess I haven't got one. Catholic tastes. But this person, who is superbly funny and smart and talented, is mine . . .

ANTON Yes, well, look, I don't see why you have to actually get—

KATIE *(over him, pleading but laughing)* Anton! I have no parents, I made a terrible choice the last time, you swore, you always said to me, you always said, "If ever you should again decide to even contemplate the prospect of marriage, please ask me first . . ."

ANTON I did say that. *(enjoying himself)* Yes. Well, I think you're rushing. Forgive me. Yes. I do. I like that I am being consulted, yes, it's only correct. After all, you're both imbeciles when it comes to romance.

KATIE That's true, it's why I'm asking your permission. Sir. I need your approval.

ANTON Live together—why do you want to change things? Especially with this depressive, complicated deeply fraught depressive creature here.

SANDY That's outrageous; how dare you!

ANTON The moods! The blackness! The terrible seriousness! AND the taste in art! All those German expressionist prints! Jesus. A Beckmann and a woodcut of a dead naked German anorexic in every room, you want to live with that?

SANDY *(laughing)* I'm not all dark and depressive—I am light, I am—well, yes, so, so I have darkness and sadness in me, but who doesn't? There is laughter and joy too! Do I not dance with happiness and sing?

He dances and sings elegantly around the room; they laugh and then applaud.

ANTON *(over Sandy's display, turns to Katie)* You want to marry Hermes Pan . . . ? *(now serious)* May I ask one question, since— are we actually being truly honest or is this just three-in-the-morning champagne-and-spaghetti euphoria?

SANDY   The latter.

ANTON   Is she aware of your past?

There is silence for a moment. A shrug from Sandy and then one from Katie.

KATIE   Ah. Is that what this is? You know I am.

ANTON   Okay. Well, I mean, it's not a secret. You know, it's no secret that we slept together seventeen years ago. This man and I. It is no secret . . .

SANDY *(dry)*   Now, Anton: How on earth could it possibly be a secret?

ANTON *(knows exactly where this is headed)*   All right, enough. Yes.

SANDY   I mean . . . *(laughing, pushing through)* Well, how? I mean—you have told everyone, you have told everyone in the tristate area and Capri too—milkmen, dental hygienists, traffic officers, librarians, congressmen, electricians—of your marvelous seduction of the straight little tortured Jewish boy from Princeton, and the wonderful months from November to February in '62 and '63. *(He triumphantly looks at the wine bottles on the bar and picks one up.)* Your last great romance.

ANTON   Hardly. Please.

SANDY   Your last stab at real love.

ANTON   You? Please. You would love to think so.

SANDY   Yes.

ANTON *(to Katie, pointing at Sandy)*   This is what you want? This unfathomable pool of narcissism?

SANDY *(waving a bottle of red)*   I'm going to drink this.

ANTON   He's unpredictable!

SANDY *(does so; suddenly serious)* Look. My past is open, I have never hidden it. I would never be here if it were not for the fact that with Katie, I am able to be honest, which is all I care about. This I know: I love this woman, Anton, and I am happy, and I want to spend the rest of my life with her. Do you know why I slept with you? Because I thought I was falling in love with you; it's not lust with me, it's never been—but I really fell in love with her. AND this is the actual, real deal, not just some fever—dream.

There is silence.

ANTON *(a sigh of resignation)* Well. Then we must have a toast. *(He solemnly raises his glass. The others follow.)* To my two best friends: You have my approval, which you hardly needed, and you have my love, which of course you do need. I am so happy for both of you.

They drink. They kiss. Katie wipes her eyes, she is crying.

KATIE It's three in the morning—we're too old for this. I'll close up the back. God, I do love you . . . *(She exits. There is silence.)*

ANTON So then.

SANDY *(still smiling)* Yeah, so then. Thank you for the paterfamilias routine. God. "Is she aware of your past." You're like a fucking lawyer.

ANTON You're quite welcome. But honestly. *(serious)* Vis-à-vis men, I have never asked you: Was I the last?

There is a moment. This is hard.

SANDY No. *(wry, and not without apology; gently)* Dr. Schiffman was certain about this, has been, that I must not hold back, must act out when I need to, and then . . .

ANTON *(a trace of the bitterness)* Go into his sanctum and spill your guts?

48

SANDY You have so little patience for this part of my life.

ANTON I have nothing but patience for every part of your life.

SANDY *(nodding at the truthfulness of that)* Brief encounters. Not for several years. Please, may we leave it at that, old friend?

ANTON It *is* past. Isn't it? And I actually—do you mind if I ask you: Have you been with men, Sandy, while you were with her? In the past year and a half? *(Beat. Sandy shakes his head no.)* Have you thought about it?

SANDY *(smiling sadly)* Have I thought about it? Are you crazy? What do you think my struggle is? This is my battle. I don't know that it will ever go away, Anton. Of course. I think about it. But I have not acted on it.

ANTON Why not?

SANDY Because it would hurt Katie. I would have to tell her, and it would hurt her terribly.

ANTON Why not lie?

SANDY I can't lie to her. Then everything would be a lie, it would all break, and the center would not hold. It would be rust. Corrosion. It would not be the same.

ANTON *(nodding, struck by it)* Yes.

SANDY *(very serious)* I would have to tell her, and I couldn't, because to do so would be to cause her to suffer. So I have put it away because I really do love her. That part of my life—is very much over. It is over. I choose this. Do you see? I choose this. Over everything else. I choose love. It is all I can do. I would die otherwise.

Katie returns from off.

KATIE Both of you. I just want to say: We are lucky. You know that? Right now—I'm happy. I am happy. I have everything, don't I? Look at this. This is perfect. *(beat)* Nobody lives like we do.

Lights out on Katie and Sandy

ANTON Perfect.

Blackout

SCENE FOUR

ANTON Yes. Once he was married, all of Sandy's raging internal wars had been more or less won. It seemed.

Yes. It was in the 1980s that he relaxed. Happiness deepened and sharpened his instincts for the work he did. Katie became well-known, beloved in New York, writing two terrific cookbooks and giving sold-out, highly coveted classes at the restaurant.

And their home! A gorgeous white living room, comfortable, piled with books and flooded with light! It was one of those places you just want to be in, and I spent a lot of time there with Sandy, Katie, and Sam, my magnificent godson, growing into a wise, clever, funny, and bold boy, adored by his mother, cherished by his stepfather.

And then Burt happened.

I don't want to bore you with facts, as they were exhaustively reported for the benefit of all. The press gloated over, and endlessly explored the thrilling "circumstances" surrounding Burt Sarris and his rather predictable, Icarus-like fall. And suicide. They made fun of the young movie stars, rock stars, and Hollywood agents who lost fortunes to Burt; poor Burty—he attempted to staunch the flow from the upper reaches of his clientele with the money from the quote "nonfamous, noncelebrities" . . . Who collapsed. Rather like dominoes. Bang. Bang. Bang. *(He takes a deep breath and gets his bearings.)*

In November of the new century's first year . . . down go the Meyersons, the Bermans, the Golds, the Orrs—these ex-clients of Sandy's, were now dispossessed—stripped of privilege wandering in the new American fiscal diaspora—like all the other poor shmucks—wondering where their good luck had gone . . . *(beat)* Yes. There is no more money. Sandy's personal fortune of seventy-five million dollars to staunch the flow, gone! The house on West Tenth Street, gone. The few remaining pieces of art, a tiny island in Maine, all gone . . . The creditors took it all.

Beat. Sigh. The lights are changing slowly.

ANTON *(cont.)*   Right. Let me take you back a year.

It is February 2001, the night my story began . . . remember? It is very late, or very early in the morning, two A.M. Sandy has just left Burt's, yes, just left unaware that Burt has taken his advice and killed himself. Earlier that day, there had been a spate of wild phone action, followed by frantic meetings with the vengeful lawyers of the panicked ex-clients of Ovid who felt they had been handed over to Burt Sarris very much like lambs to the slaughter.

SCENE FIVE
FEBRUARY 2001

The Sonnenberg home. Late night. There is a suitcase, a suit or two on a chair, a few pieces of clothing. Katie is watching Sandy.

KATIE   I don't understand what you're telling me. This is hundreds of millions of dollars you're talking about. And you think you can repay all the money he lost? You can't just go off on some unplanned mission to—For God's sake, would you give me time to catch up to you?

SANDY *(over her)*   No. No. We have resources in Lugano which I've kept safe, and by liquidating, I can make a gesture of good faith and at least give my people something. To show them that I'm a good man.

KATIE   I don't want you to go! And you do not need to demonstrate that you're good.

SANDY   I'm not, no. I'm not good. I was an idiot, I stood there and let Burt steal everything they had so he could pay them back, his movie stars. I was an idiot, Katie.

KATIE   You can't—expect me to let you go off in this state—I'm going to go with you.

SANDY   No.

Sandy puts a shirt in his suitcase, and suddenly, with a violent surge of energy, Katie rushes to it and flings it across the room.

KATIE   No! Actually—that's not good enough! No! You have to talk to me! Yes! Look at me! You must tell me. Your silence! The only thing that happens is that I imagine the worst!

SANDY *(very quietly)*   Which is what?

KATIE   You tell me! An affair? A whole series of lies? What? Christ—you owe me more—okay? You owe me more than a silent—you know—flight to try and—Jesus. *(She is crying. She hits him.)* This is it—! I never demand—I never intrude—what? Why? I don't know what has happened. I don't—you know—I've watched you become more and more absent, remote, sad, so sad, always so sad, no matter what I do, and my heart is breaking, Sandy! My heart is breaking!

Sandy holds her, and kisses her.

SANDY *(quietly)*   You've got to trust that nothing is going to—that I love you, I'm going to fix it, I haven't known what to say because I don't know what happened, how I let it happen, what it was, I don't know, please, I love you . . .

Katie sits down.

KATIE   What do I do with that? What good does that do us? Your loving me like this? I mean—it's—I assume you two had some sort of affair—I mean—you know—sex—is what happens to everybody—that's what happens to everybody but if you're going to continue to insult me by total exclusion—Talk to me! *(beat)* I know your appetites must have gotten the best of you—you think I care about that? *(beat)* Did you fall in love with Burt Sarris?

SANDY   I never fell in love with him! I just . . . I just . . . why do I need to—why do I need to—

KATIE *(furious)*   Do you think I'm stupid? Do you? People have bodies, I know that, people tell lies, I know that. I'm one of them! *(screaming)* Stop being your father's fucking son!

SANDY   I've done everything not to lead my father's life.

KATIE   No you haven't.

And silence.

SANDY   I've gone a long way down this road, Katie. I have to find my way back. You can't push me one way or the other; I have to find my own way back.

KATIE   I don't know whether I've failed you or failed myself. Both. Probably.

SANDY *(Sandy sits and picks up a piece of paper which has been sitting on the counter.)*   We have to deal with actions now. Katie. Please listen: I set up an escrow account. I want to place all of our assets, yours and mine, together, it will be seen as a gesture, irrefutably so, of undeniable good faith. You would have to put in the restaurant—the building—which is worth twelve or so— you would have to put that in.

KATIE   And that will help?

SANDY   Everything will help. It's over four hundred million lost.

KATIE That's some expensive silence.

SANDY I'll get it back, Katie.

Sandy hands her a pen. In silence, she signs.

KATIE There you are.

SANDY *(takes the paper; quietly)* Thank you. Katie. . . .

KATIE So while you're gone, please think about the conversation we have to have. Would you please? *(very quietly, not looking at him)* And it's probably better that it not be now—I . . . am . . . so fucking angry at you.

He goes. Lights fade on Katie. From off there is the harsh blaring ring of a doorbell.

ANTON *(to us)* And thus it was done. She handed over our glorious little restaurant and we were ruined. And then, a few hours later, around seven, I was awakened. *(beat)* I had taken a sleeping pill, so it took quite a bit of banging and ringing to get me up.

The lights fade on the Sonnenberg town house.

SCENE SIX

Up on Anton's apartment—the same as in Act Two, forty years ago. It is the next morning. The ringing of the doorbell for a long time, and then Anton goes to the buzzer.

She is in the apartment.

KATIE They were having an affair, weren't they? But for how long—and—

ANTON I took a quaalude. I am not—

KATIE You have to tell me, you're my friend.

ANTON *(slurred)* Yes. Well. I know—I'm *his* friend too. And I refuse to discuss him.

KATIE Of course. You know it's easier to betray me because you think I'll forgive you! But you're wrong, you're wrong, you should have told me—you chose him over me! *(beat)* But why wouldn't you? Because you're still in love with him—isn't that right? You never let it go—Jesus, Anton! Tell me the truth? Is that it? You're still in love with him?

ANTON After all this time? It's not love; it's a condition, it's . . . a malady.

She sits down on the sofa and cries. Anton goes to hold her.

KATIE How stupid. *(beat)* How fucking stupid, to have the whole of your life resting under a secret . . . And I knew. Somehow. "Nothing could be this good." I don't think I can do it, live like that, I can't take him back now and I can't bear to look at you— I've lost everything, I've lost both of you, it's all gone, I could have been told. I wouldn't have liked it, but it would have been true. My son is a homosexual and I have nothing but love for him, I understand it! *(beat)* I would have understood, had I just been told! *(She hits him hard in the chest. He lets her. Beat; quietly.)* You knew. Was it a secret compact? A fag thing? It's almost worse, losing you.

ANTON Please forgive me.

KATIE I don't have to! I don't care to! I won't make it better for either of you—!

She cries and cries. He holds her as the lights fade on her. We are on deck with Anton.

ANTON *(He stands up, adjusting his collar against the wind and salt.)* It was in *Lolita* that Nabokov's Humbert Humbert explained his parents' death thusly: "Picnic, comma, lightning." *(beat)* "Sandy disappears, comma, unable to find money in dubious foreign banks, comma, all assets seized, wife frantic, comma, wife heartbroken, comma, *(beat)* Wife gets sick." *(beat)* Katie. Katie waiting by the phone, Katie frantic. Katie being held up by Sam and me, Katie unable to find her husband, Katie left desolate, Katie half mad, Katie . . . poor Katie. There are no words to describe this. The flights to Europe. The just missing him. The first letter from him asking for some time alone. Let's skip through and past all that, please, please, please. *(beat)* Let's move to the second letter. The Paris letter. *(beat)* It is February 2002. Katie is at Mount Sinai, the day hospital, where she has just completed her third and final cycle of chemotherapy, which she has done every Tuesday. Cancer, comma, ovarian, comma, metastasized, period. It has been a year since Sandy vanished somewhere in Europe. There are still questions to be asked of him, still money owed. Still he refuses to come back until every cent has been repaid, and still he refuses to see Katie. Still.

SCENE SEVEN

Mount Sinai Hospital. Katie, Sam, and Anton. She holds a letter in her hand. She is shaking. She has on sunglasses and a beautiful scarf over her head.

ANTON I got your message; are you all right?

KATIE I got this, this letter . . . He's in Paris. He's in Paris now.

She holds out a piece of paper. Lights up on a desk. Sandy, unshaven and unkempt, a bottle of scotch before him.

KATIE Dearest Katie, I shall not come back until I am fully clear on what happened. You must make no attempt to see me.

SANDY Until Burt, I was always faithful. His charm and his ease rendered me helpless. But at a certain point, the two decades of denying those impulses just caught up to me. In March of 2000 our relationship became physical . . .

Lights fade—Lights up on Burt's loft. Burt and Sandy. Portfolios and annual reports.

BURT The issue keeps being this deep xenophobic wall that they have! It keeps coming up! I keep hitting it! Ow! Again and again—you know, man . . . ? *(He is laughing.)* You have such great—the scent. It's—like lemon and green tea and medicinal. What is it? What?

SANDY *(quietly)* I'm not sure I get this Texas thing.

BURT Are you going to give me a bottle of that?

SANDY We can not smell the same. Some things are private.

BURT What they've done in Houston is to—think of a beehive, Sandy, okay? A beehive that has been renovated and turned into a kind of elaborate, and sophisticated financial department store. A Bendel's. Who says we can't smell the same? Who made that rule? You have so many rules. They are able to control prices. They control the price of energy in California. That's what they do. *(He puts on a record.)* And I need you to somehow convey to them—the sacred clients . . . that it's okay to let me do it. They have to understand. The tribe. No more waspophobic shudders at me.

SANDY Who are you?

BURT Who are you?

Burt and Sandy kiss.

Lights down on Burt's loft.

KATIE I attempted so many times to end it. I failed in that respect as well.

SANDY I have something for you and Sam that will make this time easier, but I cannot send it through the mail, for reasons you will later understand.

KATIE I have made you suffer. I cannot expect forgiveness; even if you could, I would be unable to do so myself. Paris is silent. I know nobody, I speak no French, I am alone. I cannot see you, but if Anton could come over, he could serve as messenger in this very important business.

SANDY Oh, Katie. Why do people lie within a perfect life?

KATIE Why do people cheat when they are in love and unbearably happy?

SANDY I loved holding you at night.

KATIE I loved talking at four in the morning.

SANDY And I loved you when we made love.

KATIE I loved what you allowed and how open your heart was.

Katie cannot read any more; she hands the letter to Sam.

KATIE *(to Anton)* You'll go.

ANTON You want me to go to Paris.

KATIE Bring him back.

ANTON A terribly bad idea.

KATIE I'm not begging, Anton. I need to see him. You cannot tell him that I'm sick.

SAM He should know.

KATIE I don't want that to be a factor. Anton, you owe me this. This is what I require of you. You owe me this, and do not make me sit here, I am nauseated as it is, and tell you precisely why you owe me this. I'll be right back; wait for me here.

She gets up. Sam helps her rise. They cross the stage.

ANTON Katie, I don't think—

KATIE Don't you understand? I miss my husband. I miss him. I want him.

She exits.

SAM You'll go.

Sam exits.

ANTON *(quietly)* A newspaper never sufficiently tells the real story of a tragedy. How could it? We live in something called an "information age," but not in an age of meaning. Somehow all the intelligence is scrupulously drained on its way to us and by the time it reaches us, it's bleached and sterile. But, the real story is made up of awful quiet moments, late night silences, tears and teacups and wordless drives on hidden roads, all alone. The real story is made up of privacy and ancient sorrows, and bright light in empty lots, not recent events, it is in fathers and mothers and muffled sounds in other rooms, and in what is forgotten.

Beat. Simply. He looks at a piece of paper.

ANTON *(cont.)* For instance, the following obituary, from the *New York Times. (Beat. He reads.)* "Kathleen Arlen, chef, author of cookbooks, has died at fifty-six of cancer. Katie, who began her career in New York at the late lamented Le Singe d'Or, opened her own restaurant, Brasserie Arlen, in 1976, in the West Village. Like Le Singe, it was a convivial haven for artists and writers. She is survived by her son, Sam, and her second husband, investment banker Sanford Sonnenberg."

I was with Katie when she died. The Paris Letter was on the nightstand. She had, I discovered, spared me one paragraph:

"Katie, the night I left, you asked me if I was in love with Burt Sarris. I never was but now I'm ready to admit, I was always in love with Anton. I needed him close. I needed to know that he was still in love with me, I needed that power. I could not give it up, even as Schiffman told me I could and as I told Anton our affair had been merely a youthful experiment.

Also, as we aged, his loneliness—all the things he did not have—seemed to justify the reasons I walked away from him in 1963. Shameful, I know, but if he were happy without me, if he were fulfilled, I would have died."

The day after Katie's funeral, I left for Paris.

SCENE EIGHT
TWO DAYS LATER

Lights shift to Sandy's very shabby atelier apartment in Paris. A mattress on the floor, a simple wooden desk, a hot plate and a red armchair with the stuffing coming out as though the chair had been stabbed; indeed, stuffing is spilled on the floor. Anton and Sandy stand across from each other. Sandy is unshaven and agitated. Anton puts a bag down on the table.

SANDY Really, you're not staying long so don't bother sitting.

ANTON Ah. Really? I'm not . . . ? *(He sits. Sandy shakes his head.)* Sandy, the last thing anyone wants is to add to your pain, but I've had to walk through a fucking third-world maze to get to this . . . *(beat)* . . . charm-filled squat of yours.

SANDY In 1960, on a trip to Europe, my mother left some diamonds. In a deposit box in Lugano.

ANTON Lugano. Lovely town.

SANDY They were part of the original lot which set up the Sonnenbergs in America. There were a couple hundred. Now there are five. They're for Katie and Sam. I'd offer you one, but I know you wouldn't take it. *(He tosses a small envelope to Anton, who looks inside.)*

ANTON Yes. The mythical Sonnenberg diamonds. They're lovely. *(He takes one out.)*

SANDY Tell her to take them to Grossbard and Sons; the old man will recognize 'em.

And—and—they should not let him spend time thinking about—they're worth half a million—if he tries to screw with her I'll fuck him so—

ANTON Sandy—you're not well—I mean, look at you! You're ragged—you're—you need help.

SANDY Help?

ANTON *(over him)* and I would like to at least be able to—

SANDY Oh, help? Help? Psychiatry? Hey—wouldn't you say that—you know—I've had more than enough psychiatry in my lifetime? Aren't I the product of—you think I've had some sort of massive psychic break but this is the first moment of clarity I've had in years—perhaps in my life . . .

ANTON Yes? And tell me, does it feel good, this so-called clarity?

SANDY You think I don't know what I've done? I know! It's the only question I ask myself—"What would drive a man to destroy the only happiness he's ever, ever known?" And you have an opinion, don't you? Is it that I lived "a life of repression and denial"? Because—that's been your fucking position on me for forty years. C'mon, Anton man. Hey. Say it. You know you want to. I'm giving you permission. Say it.

ANTON What?

SANDY "I told you so." Go ahead. You must have rehearsed it. Go on and fucking say it! You've been dying to, you've waited all this time—say it—!

ANTON *(emphatic)* Yes. Yes. Yes. I. Told. You. So.

Anton is slightly stunned by the anger with which that comes out. Sandy smiles.

SANDY Now, don't you feel better? "I told you so."

Anton is somewhat undone. After a moment. His hands shake; he extracts a bottle of bourbon from his bag.

ANTON I'm sorry. Should—could we have a drink—? It may—help calm—my nerves are—Listen. I brought you—I brought you—I thought you might like a bottle . . . It's your brand. I suspect hard to get here.

SANDY Oh, I miss that. That American taste.

ANTON Are there glasses or is there only a chipped tooth mug?

Sandy hands him glasses. They are not so clean.

ANTON *(cont.)* I'll have wine; I can't handle this stuff, I'm afraid.

Sandy points to an open bottle on the table. Anton pours himself a bit. He sniffs and grimaces.

SANDY It's from a vineyard located on the edge of an industrial park right outside Paris.

ANTON Yes. I can smell the solvents.

SANDY A toast?

ANTON To old friends.

SANDY Old friends. I have to say: You don't look so great yourself, Anton.

ANTON Yes. I'm afraid I've gone to hell in a handbasket finally. I've entirely lost my looks this year. We all have.

SANDY New York. How is . . . ?

ANTON Ah. Well. New York. As you may have heard, we had a bit of a setback last year, but things are getting better.

SANDY You don't have to be entirely sarcastic, I do get some news.

ANTON It was our blitz. The Mayor was like the Queen Mum; it was very moving. I found it sort of impossible to hate him suddenly, he kept making me cry, I'd watch the man on TV and start sobbing. It must be something of a relief not to have radio or television.

SANDY   I am trying to reduce it to the bare essentials. Just these four walls . . .

ANTON   No telephone to jangle the nerves. No doorbell. No name on the door. Have to be met at a corner, where you fend off muggers. No way to reach you here in the picturesque Algerian Quarter, next to—what is it? A goat abattoir downstairs, the call to prayer to gently remind you of God a couple times a day. I think it shows a great deal of . . .

SANDY   ". . . Flair"? *(beat, smiles)* I told you not to try and goad or shame me, darling, it don't work no more. *(all business, trying to hurry and not forget)* As of today, there's two million dollars in the Sonnenberg Fund for Education. Tell Sam the creditors cannot touch it.

ANTON   Two million, go on.

SANDY *(beat)*   I miss her horribly. Is she all right? I miss her so much, Anton. And even now she doesn't hate me? How is that possible.

Sandy, with very shaky hands, pours another glass of bourbon and drinks. He sits down on the arm chair.

ANTON   Her hating you? Is that what you were after? *(gently)* You know her better than I. Her evolution is as complete as is humanly possible, I think.

   She has told me to make sure to reassure you that she forgives you and that you must not forget that. *(beat)* Whenever you are ready, she will be there. She will be ready to meet you; she has all the time in the world. She knows you love her.

SANDY   And has that love done anyone any good?

ANTON   No. Quite frankly. Your love is in fact a very malign kind of love. My only wish is that your Dr. Schiffman could see you now. I'd love to bring him here and ask him what he thinks.

SANDY   What would he think? Jesus! *(a hysterical laugh)*

ANTON   And all this because you fell in love with Burt.

SANDY   *(with emphatic certitude)*   Never. Not even for a minute, he just smelled right to me at the time.
   God. All those years with Schiffman, all that kindness, that gentle paternal wisdom in his Upper East Side office . . . and for what.
   The worst part of all of it is living to see an age where my shame, which I cherished like a magic ring, is now completely irrelevant. A joke. The whole world is gay now and it's fine!

ANTON   I told you so.

SANDY   BUT, let me tell *you* something: Let's say I'd done what I'd wanted—forty years ago. If I'd spent a life with you—or—as an openly gay man . . . yes. You wanna know what? I'd have been just as unhappy, just as sad, just as despairing. That's my curse, that's my wound . . .

The call to prayer can be heard from a local mosque.

ANTON   We'll never know, will we? We will never know.

More Muslim prayers waft in.

SANDY   They pray five or six times a day . . . I use it to count the hours. I am so tired. *(beat)* I think I'm going to close my eyes for a moment. This time of year, Paris is dark at four.

ANTON   Is it, yes. Huh . . . ?

SANDY   *(focusing; pulling himself awake)*   Anton. Please. I'm so glad you came to me.

ANTON   Sandy.

SANDY *(beat)* I think now—deep down—I would like to go home. I want to go home. Please.

Sandy closes his eyes. The light changes; shadows get longer. The call to prayer continues.

ANTON *(with great compassion)* Sandy. I was there when you told Burt to kill himself.

Beat.

SANDY You were there?

Sandy is curled up on the bed. He peers at Anton.

ANTON I was there. *(beat)* Yes. When you told him it would be better if he killed himself, when you decreed it—I was there. *(Beat. Sandy stirs; he tries to get up but is too tired.)*

SANDY . . . Anton? I can't . . . *(He tries to get up, but is too weak. He focuses for a moment.)* Oh, Anton.

The lights change.

SCENE NINE

NOVEMBER 1962

Light up on Young Sandy. He has on an overcoat, which has snow on it— it's clearly cold as hell. He is smiling, widely, when he sees Anton—old Anton, who is holding Sandy's hand as he loses consciousness.

YOUNG SANDY Anton! God, I'm late! Am I late? I am so late.

ANTON Not yet.

YOUNG SANDY Everyone else went in!

ANTON It's cold—

YOUNG SANDY I know—! I walked across the park. Everything is freezing up all of a sudden, you can see it happening; things just go jelled and then syrupy right in front of you—and then stop moving! What time's the movie?

ANTON I can't believe you never saw *Funny Face.*

YOUNG SANDY Well, you're showing me! You're showing me everything!

ANTON I'm holding some things back, my boy.

YOUNG SANDY *(laughing)* I saw you standing there from a block away and I . . .

ANTON You what?

YOUNG SANDY . . . had ideas. About later.

ANTON Did you?

YOUNG SANDY *(grinning, excited)* Ideas. Yes! Big ideas with—with lots of complicated phases—which cannot be discussed at this time!
Involving rope and wine and circuses and pillows and rooftops you don't know about and the pool in the basement of my mom's friend Carol's house while she's on the *Queen Mary* but I have the keys—!

ANTON Then I'll leave it to you.

YOUNG SANDY Let's go on in. *(Beat. A moment. He is staring at Anton.)* Look at this city? It's . . . *(beat)* We own it. Nobody else. It's all ours. Everything is all ours.

The lights fade on Young Sandy. Back up on the Paris flat.

ANTON *(gently)* You had so much power. You had so much power. A monster's charm. *(beat)* Go to sleep. All you have to do is listen, kitty cat, keep your eyes closed and listen, Sandy. *(beat)* Look at yourself. You have lived in bad faith, Sandy. An entire life lived in bad faith. But soon that will be gone. It will all be gone soon.

And so it goes. An entire bottle of quaaludes ground very, very fine and mixed into the bourbon.

Beat. He walks to the lip of the stage, to the very edge and looks out.

ANTON *(cont.)*   And that is how one becomes a killer. A killer of a certain class. I suppose that's what I am, but I think it was euthanasia, really. It is only mercy. Only. His lies had become more important than his love, and the family he wanted so badly was ruined, so what was left for him? It is only mercy. *(beat)* I have a few days in Paris, I will sit in the Place des Vosges and the Luxembourg Gardens, eat dinner alone and wander the Clingnancourt flea market before I go home to New York. *(beat)* I shall go back, and be a friend to, and even parent to my beautiful Sam and perhaps he will even find some kind of happiness, some new kind of happiness, not yet quantified, or measured, or commodified, with another person or not. I shall watch over him. . . . *(beat)* . . . For as long as God allows. *(beat)* Good night.